My Little Golden Book About
SHARKS

By BONNIE BADER • Illustrated by STEPH LABERIS

The editors would like to thank Paul L. Sieswerda, executive director at gothamwhale.com, for his assistance in the preparation of this book.

For Pixie —S.L.

A GOLDEN BOOK • NEW YORK

Educators and librarians, for a variety of teaching tools, visit us at
RHTeachersLibrarians.com
Library of Congress Control Number: 2015935297
ISBN 978-1-101-93092-2 (trade) — ISBN 978-1-101-93093-9 (ebook)
Printed in the United States of America
10 9 8 7 6 5 4 3 2

P9-DBY-577

great white shark

thresher shark

whale shark

hammerhead shark

oceanic whitetip shark

Deep in the ocean, sharks swim.
A shark is a type of fish.
Sharks have swum the oceans for hundreds
of millions of years. They were around long
before the dinosaurs!

The shark's body—from the inside to the outside—is perfect for swimming.

Sharks don't have bones. Their bodies are supported by cartilage. Cartilage feels soft and bendable, not hard, like bones. You have cartilage in your ears and nose.

Cartilage helps sharks turn and bend easily.

A shark's pectoral fins help it steer up and down.
Its pelvic fins help keep it steady.
Its dorsal fin helps it keep its balance in the water.
Some sharks have two dorsal fins.

second dorsal fin

pelvic fin

thresher shark

first dorsal fin

gill slits

pectoral fin

A shark's tail gives it power as it swims. The thresher shark has the longest tail of all sharks. Water contains oxygen, which we all breathe. As a shark swims, water flows into its mouth and out its gill slits. The gills take oxygen from the water so that the shark can breathe.

A shark's skin feels rough. The skin is covered with tiny sharp points called denticles. Denticles help protect the shark's skin, and even keep it clean!

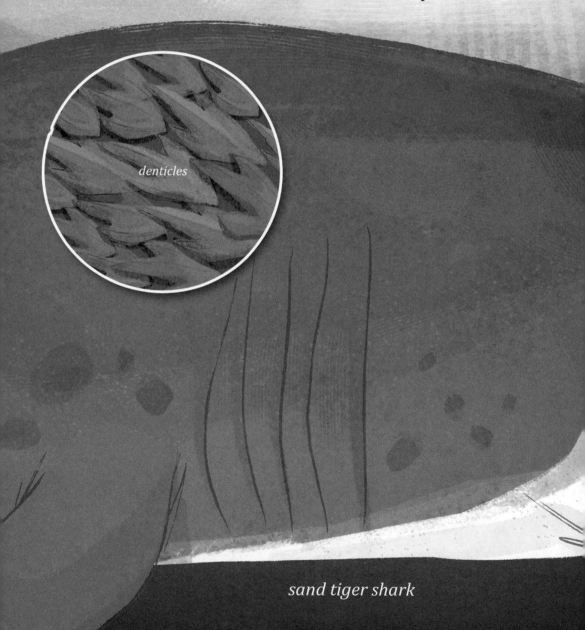

denticles

sand tiger shark

Sharks have rows and rows of teeth in their powerful jaws. When one tooth falls out, a tooth from a row in the back moves up and takes its place.

It is dark way down in the ocean. But sharks have excellent eyesight. They have a great sense of smell, too.

There are more than
four hundred different
kinds of sharks. And
scientists are still
discovering new ones.
   Here comes the fastest
shark in the world!

The shortfin mako can swim as fast as sixty
miles per hour. That's as fast as some cars
drive on a highway! This shark is a good hunter
and likes to eat squid and sea turtles. It can
leap as high as twenty feet to catch a big fish!

While some sharks chase their food out of the water, others find their food at the bottom of the sea. The angel shark's flat body and wide pectoral fins make it easy for it to lie on the ocean floor and snatch any fish that swim by.

Like the angel shark, the wobbegong has a flat body. But it also has markings on its skin that look like rocks, and frills that look like seaweed. It can blend into coral reefs without being seen.

This sneaky shark can creep up on a crab crawling by. *Snap!* Dinnertime!

Unlike most sharks, nurse sharks have smooth skin. They can grow up to fourteen feet long. Their barbels, which look like whiskers, help them find and taste food on the ocean floor. And their strong jaws help them crush and eat shellfish.

Another shark that likes to live near the dark ocean floor is the rare goblin shark. Its long snout acts like a metal detector when a tasty fish or squid comes along. Then out, out, out slide the jaws!

While the goblin shark doesn't like the light, the lantern shark *makes* its own light, in its skin, to help attract prey. But the light on the shark's belly also helps it become invisible! The lantern shark shines light on the water around it, making the water shine and the shark look dark. *Whoosh!* A bigger fish swims by and doesn't see the lantern shark at all!

What is that shark with the dark stripes? It's a tiger shark pup. This baby will grow to be fourteen to twenty feet long and will weigh around one thousand pounds. Tiger sharks will eat any kind of fish, shark, or animal it can find. It has even been known to eat pieces of boats, clothing, tires, and books!

egg case

swellshark mother

egg

Sharks have babies in three different ways.

Some pups are born alive from their mother. These types of sharks can have more than one hundred pups at one time!

Other shark mothers lay eggs, and the babies hatch. Maybe you've come across an empty egg case on the beach. Some people call that a mermaid's purse.

A zebra shark lays eggs, but the baby hatches inside its mother and lives on egg yolk until it's ready to be born. At that time, the shark mother gives birth to a tiny zebra shark.

The baby is dark brown, with stripes like a zebra. As it gets older, it also develops spots, making it look like a zebra-leopard!

The lemon shark's yellowish color helps it blend into the sandy seafloor. A lemon shark mother gives birth to her babies in the water. She can have between four and seventeen pups at a time.

Here comes one of the most amazing sharks—
the great white. This shark can grow to be more than
sixteen feet long and weigh more than two thousand
pounds. It can smell a single drop of blood! The great
white will go above water to catch seals, sea lions,
otters, and turtles in its huge jaws.

This shark doesn't look like another animal—
it looks like a tool! Its head is shaped like a hammer.
Hammerheads' eyes are on the sides of their heads,
which makes it easier for them to find food all around
them. And their flat heads act like metal detectors,
sensing fish hiding in the sand. This helps them find
stingrays, their favorite food.

Some people think that all sharks attack humans. This is not true. The chance that a shark will attack you is very small. Actually, humans cause more harm to sharks than sharks cause to humans. It is important to protect sharks.

Deep in the ocean, sharks swim.
Who knows what kind of shark
will be discovered next!